CONTENTS

2

CHAPTER 1 • Understanding Addition and Subtraction

Mixed Review 1
Addition 2
Addition Patterns 3
Count On 4
Related Addition Facts 5
Problem-Solving Strategy: Write an Addition Sentence 6
Subtraction 7
Subtraction Patterns 8
Count Back 9
Related Subtraction Facts 10
Problem-Solving Strategy: Write a Subtraction Sentence . . . 11
Problem Solving: Read to Understand 12

CHAPTER 2 • Addition and Subtraction Strategies

Mixed Review 13
Add 9 14
Make a 10 15
Three or More Addends 16
Subtract with Doubles 17
Count Up to Subtract 18
Subtract 9 19
Problem-Solving Strategy: Choose the Operation 20
Related Facts 21
Fact Families 22
Problem Solving: Choose a Strategy 23

CHAPTER 3 • Place Value and Graphing

Mixed Review 24

Tens and Ones 25

Numbers to 50 26

Numbers to 100 27

Order to 100 28

Skip-Count by Fives and Tens 29

Skip-Count by Twos 30

Odd and Even 31

Mixed Review 32

Compare Numbers 33

Problem-Solving Strategy: Use Logical Reasoning 34

Bar Graphs 35

Pictographs 36

Use Pictographs 37

Problem Solving: Use a Graph 38

CHAPTER 4 • Money

Mixed Review 39

Quarters 40

Counting Quarters 41

Problem-Solving Strategy: Use Guess and Test 42

Dollars 43

Dollars and Cents 44

Comparing Money 45

Problem Solving: Make Change 46

CHAPTER 5 • Telling Time

Mixed Review 47

Hour and Half Hour 48

Quarter Hour 49

Mixed Review 50

More Minutes 51

Problem-Solving Strategy: Work Backward 52

Use a Calendar 53

Ordinal Numbers 54

Problem Solving: Use a Schedule 55

CHAPTER 6 • Exploring 2-Digit Addition and Subtraction

Mixed Review 56

More Mental Math 57

Mixed Review 58

Count Back by Tens 59

Mental Math 60

Problem-Solving Strategy: Solve 2-Step Problems 61

Addition Strategies 62

Subtraction Strategies 63

Problem Solving: Solve Multistep Problems 64

CHAPTER 7 • Adding 2-Digit Numbers

Mixed Review 65

More Regrouping 66

Add 2-Digit Numbers 67

More Adding 2-Digit Numbers 68

Add to Solve Problems 69

Problem-Solving Strategy: Use Estimation 70

Check Addition 71

Mixed Review 72

More Adding Money 73

Problem Solving: Choose the Method 74

CHAPTER 8 • Subtracting 2-Digit Numbers

Mixed Review 75

More Regrouping 76

Subtract 2-Digit Numbers 77

More Subtracting 2-Digit Numbers 78

Subtract to Solve Problems 79

Problem-Solving Strategy: Make a List 80

Mixed Review 81

Check Subtraction 82

Add or Subtract to Solve Problems 83

Problem Solving: Identify Extra Information 84

CHAPTER 9 • Geometry and Fractions

Mixed Review 85

Three-Dimensional Shapes 86

Two-Dimensional Shapes 87

Congruent Shapes 88

Symmetry 89

Problem-Solving Strategy: Use a Pattern 90

Mixed Review 91

Fractions 92

More Fractions 93

Fraction of a Group 94

Problem Solving: Draw a Picture 95

CHAPTER 10 • Measurement

Mixed Review 96

Inch and Foot 97

PROBLEM-SOLVING STRATEGY: WRITE A SUBTRACTION SENTENCE

✔ Read
✔ Plan
✔ Solve
✔ Look Back

Write a subtraction sentence to show your thinking.
Solve.

	Workspace
1. Bobby counts 8 fish in the fish tank. He buys 5 of them. How many fish are left in the tank? __3__ fish	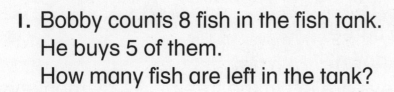
2. Tanya buys 6 boxes of bird food. She gives 4 boxes to Ann. How many boxes does Tanya have now? _____ boxes	
3. 7 children went to pet the rabbits. Then 2 children left to see the snakes. How many children stayed to pet the rabbits? _____ children	
4. Rita sees 10 kittens. 6 of the kittens have stripes. How many kittens do not have stripes? _____ kittens	

McGraw-Hill School Division

PROBLEM SOLVING: READ TO UNDERSTAND

☑ Read
☑ Plan
☑ Solve
☑ Look Back

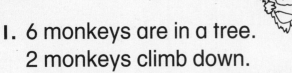

Solve.

1. 6 monkeys are in a tree.
   2 monkeys climb down.
   How many monkeys are left in the tree?   ___ monkeys

2. 8 red parrots are in the tree.
   4 blue parrots are in the tree.
   Are there more blue or red parrots?   ___ parrots

3. 12 parrots are in a tree. 6 of the parrots
   fly away. How many parrots are in the
   tree now?   ___ parrots

4. There are 2 spiders and 8 flies on a plant.
   How many more flies are there?   ___ flies

5. What strategy can you use to solve
   problem 4?

   _____

   _____

6. Write a new question for problem 4.
   Have a partner solve it.

   _____

   _____

SUBTRACT WITH DOUBLES

Solve.   Workspace

1. Pedro wrote 5 poems on Friday.
   He wrote 5 poems on Saturday.
   How many poems did he write?

   __10__ poems

   $$\begin{array}{r} 5 \\ +\;5 \\ \hline 10 \end{array}$$

2. Pedro wrote 5 poems for his friends.
   How many were not for his friends?

   _____ poems

3. Sandy has 7 red pencils and 7 blue
   pencils. How many pencils does
   she have?

   _____ pencils

4. Sandy gave away 7 of the pencils
   she had. How many pencils does
   she have left?

   _____ pencils

5. Dan had 2 books. He got 2 more.
   How many books does Dan have now?

   _____ books

 Write a subtraction problem about Dan.

_____

_____

McGraw-Hill School Division

COUNT UP TO SUBTRACT

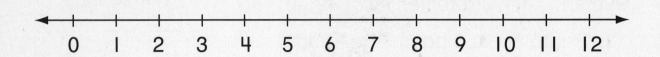

<----+----+----+----+----+----+----+----+----+----+----+----+----+---->
  0   1   2   3   4   5   6   7   8   9 10 11 12

Subtract.
Count up if you forget a fact.

1.

$$\begin{array}{r} 5 \\ -2 \\ \hline 3 \end{array}\qquad \begin{array}{r} 12 \\ -3 \\ \hline \end{array}\qquad \begin{array}{r} 7 \\ -1 \\ \hline \end{array}\qquad \begin{array}{r} 7 \\ -3 \\ \hline \end{array}\qquad \begin{array}{r} 11 \\ -6 \\ \hline \end{array}\qquad \begin{array}{r} 8 \\ -1 \\ \hline \end{array}$$

2.

$$\begin{array}{r} 10 \\ -3 \\ \hline \end{array}\qquad \begin{array}{r} 11 \\ -3 \\ \hline \end{array}\qquad \begin{array}{r} 12 \\ -3 \\ \hline \end{array}\qquad \begin{array}{r} 7 \\ -2 \\ \hline \end{array}\qquad \begin{array}{r} 9 \\ -3 \\ \hline \end{array}\qquad \begin{array}{r} 12 \\ -7 \\ \hline \end{array}$$

3.

$$\begin{array}{r} 10 \\ -2 \\ \hline \end{array}\qquad \begin{array}{r} 9 \\ -1 \\ \hline \end{array}\qquad \begin{array}{r} 8 \\ -2 \\ \hline \end{array}\qquad \begin{array}{r} 11 \\ -7 \\ \hline \end{array}\qquad \begin{array}{r} 10 \\ -1 \\ \hline \end{array}\qquad \begin{array}{r} 5 \\ -1 \\ \hline \end{array}$$

4.

$$\begin{array}{r} 11 \\ -2 \\ \hline \end{array}\qquad \begin{array}{r} 8 \\ -3 \\ \hline \end{array}\qquad \begin{array}{r} 12 \\ -5 \\ \hline \end{array}\qquad \begin{array}{r} 9 \\ -4 \\ \hline \end{array}\qquad \begin{array}{r} 11 \\ -4 \\ \hline \end{array}\qquad \begin{array}{r} 10 \\ -5 \\ \hline \end{array}$$

5.

$$\begin{array}{r} 12 \\ -6 \\ \hline \end{array}\qquad \begin{array}{r} 6 \\ -1 \\ \hline \end{array}\qquad \begin{array}{r} 9 \\ -2 \\ \hline \end{array}\qquad \begin{array}{r} 11 \\ -5 \\ \hline \end{array}\qquad \begin{array}{r} 8 \\ -4 \\ \hline \end{array}\qquad \begin{array}{r} 6 \\ -2 \\ \hline \end{array}$$

SUBTRACT 9

Subtract. Use strategies if you need help.

1.
$$
\begin{array}{r} 10 \\ -\ 9 \\ \hline \end{array}
\qquad
\begin{array}{r} 14 \\ -\ 9 \\ \hline \end{array}
\qquad
\begin{array}{r} 17 \\ -\ 9 \\ \hline \end{array}
\qquad
\begin{array}{r} 12 \\ -\ 9 \\ \hline \end{array}
\qquad
\begin{array}{r} 15 \\ -\ 9 \\ \hline \end{array}
$$

2.
$$
\begin{array}{r} 13 \\ -\ 9 \\ \hline \end{array}
\qquad
\begin{array}{r} 9 \\ -\ 9 \\ \hline \end{array}
\qquad
\begin{array}{r} 11 \\ -\ 9 \\ \hline \end{array}
\qquad
\begin{array}{r} 16 \\ -\ 9 \\ \hline \end{array}
\qquad
\begin{array}{r} 18 \\ -\ 9 \\ \hline \end{array}
$$

Solve.   Workspace

3. Susan had 15 crayons on the table. She put away 9 of them. How many crayons were still on the table?

   _____ crayons

4. Raphael made 16 cards. He mailed 9 cards to some friends. How many cards does he have now?

   _____ cards

5. Jon's class needs 12 paintbrushes. They have only 9 paintbrushes. How many more do they need?

   _ paintbrushes

Practice
20

PROBLEM-SOLVING STRATEGY: CHOOSE THE OPERATION

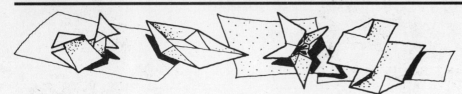

Choose addition or subtraction. Solve.

1. Yoko folded 8 paper cranes.
   Amy folded 6 paper cranes.
   How many paper cranes did
   they fold in all?

   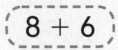

   $8 - 6$

   __14__ cranes

2. The children hung 12 drawings
   on the wall. 4 drawings fell down.
   How many drawings are left on
   the wall?

   $12 + 4$

   $12 - 4$

   _____ drawings

3. Jerry made 11 paper boats.
   7 boats were blue.
   How many boats were not blue?

   $11 + 7$

   $11 - 7$

   _____ boats

4. 7 classes saw the art show today.
   6 classes saw the art show yesterday.
   How many classes saw the art show?

   $7 + 6$

   $7 - 6$

   _____ classes

McGraw-Hill School Division

PROBLEM SOLVING: CHOOSE A STRATEGY

✔	Read
✔	Plan
✔	Solve
✔	Look Back

Show how you solve these problems.

Workspace

1. 9 children were on the swings.
5 children joined them.
How many children are on the
swings now?

_____14_____ children

2. 5 children played jump rope.
9 children played tag. How many
more children played tag?

_____ children

3. There were 17 children outside.
Then 8 of them went inside. How
many children are still outside?

_____ children

4. Write a problem about players on
a team. Have a partner solve it.

_____

_____

Name: _____

MIXED REVIEW

Make a ten. Add.

1. 7
 + 4
 = 11

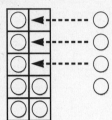

2. 6
 + 6

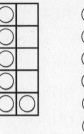

3. 8   9   6   7   8   9
 + 5   + 7   + 8   + 6   + 7   + 6

4. 6   7   9   8   8   8
 + 7   + 5   + 4   + 8   + 3   + 9

Solve.   Workspace

5. Paco collects 5 leaves.
Then he finds 8 more.
How many leaves does
he have in all? _____

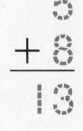

6. Rita has 9 flowers.
Then she picks 5 more.
How many flowers does
she have in all? _____

7. Ada collects 6 rocks.
Then she gets 5 more.
How many rocks does
she have in all? _____

McGraw-Hill School Division

Name:

TENS AND ONES

Draw one more cube.
Write how many tens and ones and the number.

1.

_____ tens _____ ones

_____ fourteen

2.

_____ tens _____ ones

_____ twelve

3.

_____ tens _____ ones

_____ seventeen

4.

_____ tens _____ ones

_____ eleven

5.

_____ tens _____ ones

_____ twenty

6.

_____ tens _____ ones

_____ eighteen

7.

_____ tens _____ ones

_____ thirteen

8.

_____ tens _____ ones

_____ sixteen

NUMBERS TO 50

Count. Write how many tens and ones and the number.

1.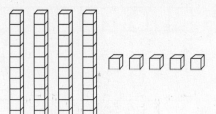

___4___ tens   ___5___ ones

___45___

2.

_____ tens   _____ ones

_____

3.

_____ tens   _____ ones

_____

4.

_____ tens   _____ ones

_____

Write how many tens and ones.

5. 30 ___3___ tens ___0___ ones

6. 11 _____ tens _____ ones

7. 15 _____ tens _____ ones

8. 23 _____ tens _____ ones

47 _____ tens _____ ones

40 _____ tens _____ ones

8 _____ tens _____ ones

33 _____ tens _____ ones

NUMBERS TO 100

Count. Write how many tens and ones and
the number.

1.

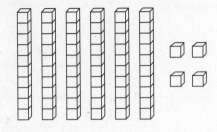

____6____ tens   ____4____ ones

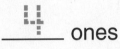

2.

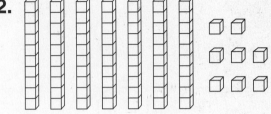

_____ tens   _____ ones

_____

3.

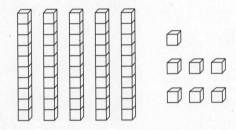

_____ tens   _____ ones

_____

4.

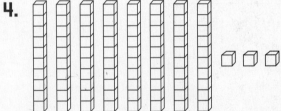

_____ tens   _____ ones

_____

Write how many tens and ones.

5. 53 ____5____ tens ____3____ ones

6. 95 _____ tens _____ ones

7. 67 _____ tens _____ ones

8. 71 _____ tens _____ ones

86 _____ tens _____ ones

70 _____ tens _____ ones

92 _____ tens _____ ones

59 _____ tens _____ ones

ORDER TO 100

Write the number that is just after.

Use mental math!

1. 48 49   51   67

2. 29   89   74

3. 55   98   59

Write the number that is just before.

4. 95 96   ___ 23   ___ 100

5. ___ 50   ___ 78   ___ 81

6. ___ 19   ___ 34   ___ 51

Write the number that is between.

7. 71 72 73   39 ___ 41

8. 68 ___ 70   94 ___ 96

McGraw-Hill School Division

SKIP-COUNT BY FIVES AND TENS

Skip-count by tens. Write the numbers.

1. 6   16   26   ___   ___   ___   ___

2. 21   31   ___   ___   ___   ___   ___

3. 17   27   ___   ___   ___   ___   ___

4. ___   ___   29   39   ___   ___   ___

5. ___   44   ___   ___   74   ___   94

Count by 5s. Draw a path.
Help the bird find the nest.

	1	14	20	10	46
6	5	7	35	40	45
18	10	29	30	15	50
25	15	20	25	26	

Name: _____

SKIP-COUNT BY TWOS

Connect the dots.
Skip-count by twos.

You may color
in your picture
when you finish.

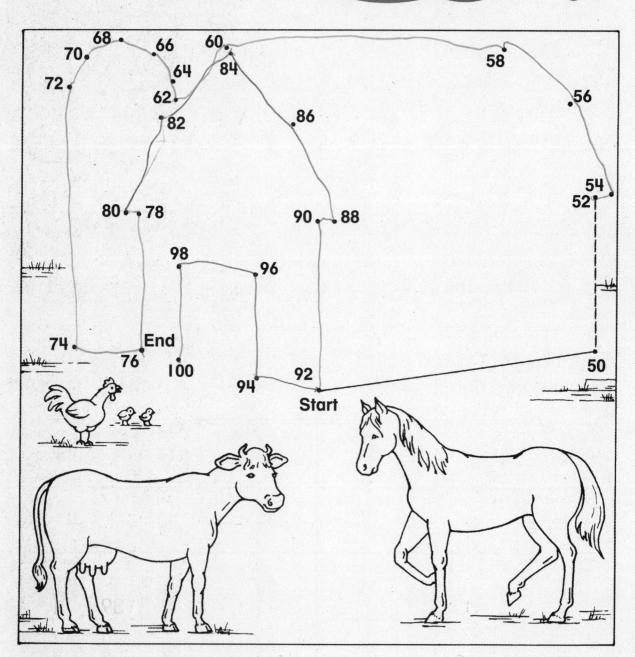

What did you draw? _____

Name: _____

ODD AND EVEN

Write *odd* or *even* for each number. You may use cubes to help.

The number is even if the train can be split into 2 equal parts.

1.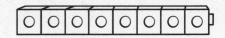

5 ___odd___   8 _____

2.

6 _____   3 _____

3.

13 _____

4.   16 _____

Make a pattern. Color the odd numbers.

1	2	3	4	5	6	7	8	9	10
11	12	13	14	15	16	17	18	19	20
21	22	23	24	25	26	27	28	29	30
31	32	33	34	35	36	37	38	39	40
41	42	43	44	45	46	47	48	49	50

MIXED REVIEW

Complete each fact family.

1.

7	2	9	9
+ 2	+ 7	− 2	− 7
9	9	7	2

2.
8	3
+ 3	+ 8
11	11
− 3	− 8

3.
5	4
+ 4	+ 5
9	9
− 4	− 5

4.
6	8
+ 8	+ 6
14	14
− 8	− 6

5.
7	6
+ 6	+ 7
13	13
− 6	− 7

6.
9	3
+ 3	+ 9
12	12
− 3	− 9

7.
5	6
+ 6	+ 5
11	11
− 6	− 5

COMPARE NUMBERS

Compare the two numbers.
Circle the correct words.

You may use
models to help.

I.   is less than

34   12

(is greater than)

2.   is less than

67   81

is greater than

---

3.   is less than

76   78

is greater than

4.   is less than

93   89

is greater than

---

5.   is less than

56   48

is greater than

6.   is less than

25   35

is greater than

---

7.   is less than

45   54

is greater than

8.   is less than

51   50

is greater than

Compare. Write $<$ or $>$.

9. 47 $<$ 51   72 ◯ 62   29 ◯ 43

10. 83 ◯ 53   91 ◯ 94   53 ◯ 36

11. 74 ◯ 92   64 ◯ 59   38 ◯ 43

12. 41 ◯ 14   79 ◯ 97   40 ◯ 39

PROBLEM-SOLVING STRATEGY: USE LOGICAL REASONING

Solve.

1. How many children collect leaves?

The number of children is less than 35.
The ones digit is greater than the tens digit.
There are 3 tens in the number.
How many children collect leaves?   ____ children

2. How many birds does Koko count?

The number of birds is greater than 60.
The ones digit is just before 6.
The number of birds is less than 70.
How many birds does Koko count? _____ birds

3. How many trees are in the yard?

The number is between 13 and 17.
The ones digit is an odd number.
How many trees in the yard? _____ trees

4. How many flowers are in the garden?

There are 6 tens in the number.
The ones digit is an even number.
The ones digit is less than 4.
How many flowers are in the garden? _____ flowers

McGraw-Hill School Division

USE PICTOGRAPHS

Here are flowers.

daisies   30
roses   20
buttercups   15

1. Decide on a title for the graph.
Complete the pictograph.

Title _____

daisies

roses

buttercups

I 🌼 means 5 flowers

Use the graph to answer these questions.

2. How many flowers does each
picture mean?   _____

3. How many more daisies than
roses are there?   _____

4. How many more daisies than
buttercups are there?   _____

5. How do you count the flowers
you drew?   _____

PROBLEM SOLVING: USE A GRAPH

✔ Read
✔ Plan
✔ Solve
✔ Look Back

The children at the Pearl River School collected cans to raise money for a science fair. The pictograph shows how many bags they were able to fill with cans.

Bags of Cans to Recycle

Week 1	🛍 🛍 🛍 🛍 🛍
Week 2	🛍 🛍 🛍
Week 3	🛍 🛍 🛍 🛍 🛍 🛍 🛍

Each 🛍 means 2 bags of cans.

Solve.

1. How many bags were collected in all? _____

2. How many bags were collected in Week 1 and Week 2 altogether? _____

3. How did you solve the problem?

_____

4. What if they collected 8 bags of cans in Week 4? How many bags would they draw on the graph? _____

5. How many more bags were collected in Week 3 than in Week 2? _____

McGraw-Hill School Division

MIXED REVIEW

Skip-count by tens. Write the numbers.

1. 10, 20, 30, _40_, _50_, _____, _____, _____

2. 7, 17, _____, _____, _____, _____, _____, _____

3. 24, 34, _____, _____, _____, _____, _____, _____

Count the dimes by tens.

4. (10¢) (20¢) (30¢)

       _____

Skip-count by fives. Write the numbers.

5. 5, 10, 15, _20_, _25_, _____, _____, _____

6. 55, 60, _____, _____, _____, _____, _____, _____,

 _____, _____

Count the nickels by fives.

7. (5¢) (10¢) (15¢)

       _____

Name: _____

QUARTERS

Count. Write how much money.

1.

| 25¢ | 35¢ | 40¢ | 45¢ | 50¢ | 51¢ | 52¢ |

_52¢_

2.

_____

3.

_____

4.

_____

5.

_____

6.

_____

Grade 2, Chapter 4, Lesson 2, Day 1, pages 139–140

Name: _____

COUNTING QUARTERS

Count. Write how much money.

1.

83¢

2.

_____

3.

_____

4.

_____

5.

_____

6.

_____

Grade 2, Chapter 4, Lesson 2, Day 2, pages 141–142

PROBLEM-SOLVING STRATEGY: USE GUESS AND TEST

✔ Read
✔ Plan
✔ Solve
✔ Look Back

Solve. You may use , or .

Workspace

9¢ + 3¢ = 12¢
8¢ + 4¢ = 12¢
7¢ + 5¢ = 12¢

1. Lulu spends 12¢.
   Which two things could she buy?

   pot and fork, can and

   flower, rake and seeds

2. Chet has 11¢ to spend.
   Which two things could he buy?

   rake, flower.

3. Emily spends 13¢.
   Which two things could she buy?

   pot flower

4. Mark has 18¢ to spend.
   Which three things could he buy?

   two flowers, hat.

McGraw-Hill School Division

DOLLARS

Count. Write how much money.

1.

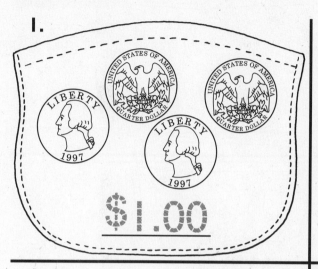

$1.00

2.

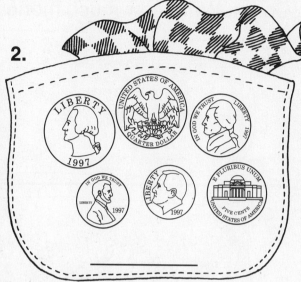

_____

3.

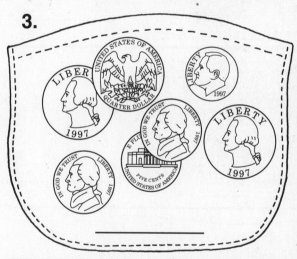

_____

4.

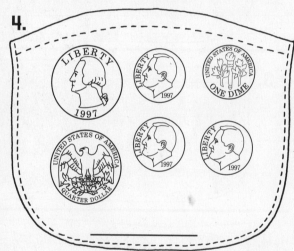

_____

5.

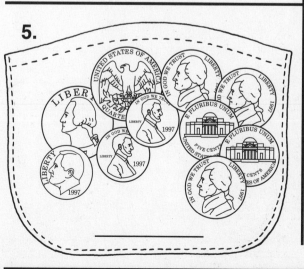

_____

6.

_____

DOLLARS AND CENTS

Count. Write how much money.

1.  $1.80

2.  1.10

3.  2.54

4. 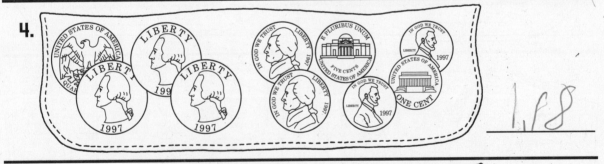 1.18

5.  3.29

Grade 2, Chapter 4, Lesson 4, Day 2, pages 151–152

McGraw-Hill School Division

COMPARING MONEY

Count. Is there enough money?
Choose *yes* or *no*.

1.

yes

$1.20   ⟨no⟩

2.

yes

_____ no

3.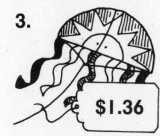

yes

_____ no

4.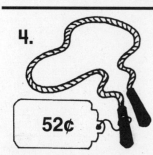

yes

_____ no

5.

yes

_____ no

PROBLEM SOLVING: MAKE CHANGE

✔ Read
✔ Plan
✔ Solve
✔ Look Back

School Store

Notebook 65¢　　**Pencils 41¢**　　**Book bag 89¢**　　**Ruler 33¢**

Use coins to count up and make change.

I. Claire bought a notebook.
She gave the clerk $1.00.
What was her change?

75¢, 85¢, 95¢, $1.00　　　　35¢

2. Leroy bought the set of pencils.
He gave the clerk 50¢.
What was his change?

_____　　_____

3. Ruby bought a book bag.
She gave the clerk $1.00.
What was her change?

_____　　_____

4. Dylan bought a ruler.
He gave the clerk 50¢.
What was his change?

_____　　_____

McGraw-Hill School Division

MIXED REVIEW

Count. Write how much money.

1.

40¢

2.

_____

3.

_____

4.

_____

5.

_____

6.

_____

7.

_____

8.

_____

HOUR AND HALF HOUR

Draw the missing minute hand to show the
same time.

1.

2.

3.

4.

5.

6.

7.

8.

9.

10.

McGraw-Hill School Division

QUARTER HOUR

Write the time.
Write the time 15 minutes later.

1.  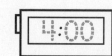 15 minutes later

2.  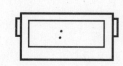 15 minutes later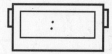

3.  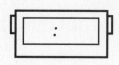 15 minutes later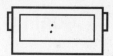

4.  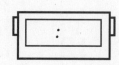 15 minutes later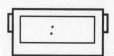

5.  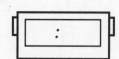 15 minutes later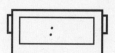

MIXED REVIEW

Add.

1.
$$\begin{array}{r} 4 \\ +7 \\ \hline 11 \end{array}$$
$$\begin{array}{r} 8 \\ +5 \\ \hline \end{array}$$
$$\begin{array}{r} 9 \\ +8 \\ \hline \end{array}$$
$$\begin{array}{r} 5 \\ +6 \\ \hline \end{array}$$
$$\begin{array}{r} 8 \\ +8 \\ \hline \end{array}$$
$$\begin{array}{r} 9 \\ +4 \\ \hline \end{array}$$

2.
$$\begin{array}{r} 8 \\ +6 \\ \hline \end{array}$$
$$\begin{array}{r} 9 \\ +7 \\ \hline \end{array}$$
$$\begin{array}{r} 7 \\ +8 \\ \hline \end{array}$$
$$\begin{array}{r} 9 \\ +5 \\ \hline \end{array}$$
$$\begin{array}{r} 6 \\ +9 \\ \hline \end{array}$$
$$\begin{array}{r} 8 \\ +3 \\ \hline \end{array}$$

3.
$$\begin{array}{r} 9 \\ +9 \\ \hline \end{array}$$
$$\begin{array}{r} 7 \\ +7 \\ \hline \end{array}$$
$$\begin{array}{r} 8 \\ +9 \\ \hline \end{array}$$
$$\begin{array}{r} 6 \\ +7 \\ \hline \end{array}$$
$$\begin{array}{r} 9 \\ +3 \\ \hline \end{array}$$
$$\begin{array}{r} 8 \\ +7 \\ \hline \end{array}$$

Subtract. Count up if you forget a fact.

4.
$$\begin{array}{r} 7 \\ -4 \\ \hline 3 \end{array}$$
$$\begin{array}{r} 10 \\ -8 \\ \hline \end{array}$$
$$\begin{array}{r} 7 \\ -6 \\ \hline \end{array}$$
$$\begin{array}{r} 11 \\ -9 \\ \hline \end{array}$$
$$\begin{array}{r} 10 \\ -7 \\ \hline \end{array}$$
$$\begin{array}{r} 9 \\ -8 \\ \hline \end{array}$$

5.
$$\begin{array}{r} 5 \\ -4 \\ \hline \end{array}$$
$$\begin{array}{r} 9 \\ -7 \\ \hline \end{array}$$
$$\begin{array}{r} 12 \\ -9 \\ \hline \end{array}$$
$$\begin{array}{r} 10 \\ -9 \\ \hline \end{array}$$
$$\begin{array}{r} 5 \\ -3 \\ \hline \end{array}$$
$$\begin{array}{r} 7 \\ -5 \\ \hline \end{array}$$

6.
$$\begin{array}{r} 8 \\ -6 \\ \hline \end{array}$$
$$\begin{array}{r} 6 \\ -5 \\ \hline \end{array}$$
$$\begin{array}{r} 11 \\ -8 \\ \hline \end{array}$$
$$\begin{array}{r} 9 \\ -6 \\ \hline \end{array}$$
$$\begin{array}{r} 6 \\ -4 \\ \hline \end{array}$$
$$\begin{array}{r} 8 \\ -7 \\ \hline \end{array}$$

MORE MINUTES

Write the time.

1.    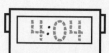   **2 minutes later**

2.    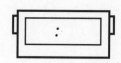   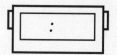   **1 minute later**

3.    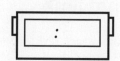   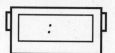   **3 minutes later**

4.    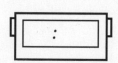   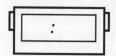   **5 minutes later**

5.    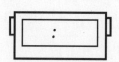   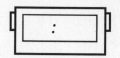   **4 minutes later**

6.    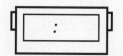   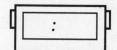   **5 minutes later**

PROBLEM-SOLVING STRATEGY: WORK BACKWARD

Solve.

1. The children got to the farm at 9:00. They were on the bus for 1 hour. What time did they get on the bus? 8:00

2. The children stopped picking apples at 12:00. They spent 2 hours picking apples. What time did they start? ___:___

3. The children saw lambs at 11:30. They saw goats 1 hour earlier. What time did they see the goats? ___:___

4. The children finished lunch at 1:30. They ate lunch for 1 hour. What time did they start lunch? ___:___

5. The children must be on the bus at 4:00. They have 2 more hours to visit. What time is it now? ___:___

McGraw-Hill School Division

PROBLEM SOLVING:
USE A SCHEDULE

✔ Read
✔ Plan
✔ Solve
✔ Look Back

Channel	11:30 A.M.	12:00 P.M.	12:30 P.M.	1:00 P.M.	1:30 P.M.
23	Movie: *Country Road*		Mary Reed Show	Buying from Home	Today's News
49	Dom's Cooking	Science Times	School Street	Learning English	Learn to Paint

Solve.

1. Which channel has all
   half-hour shows?   Channel _____49_____

2. Which show is 1 hour long?   _____

3. Can you watch both "Science Times" and
   the "Mary Reed Show"? Explain.

   _____

   _____

4. Solve Elena's problem. Explain your answer.
   Elena turned on Channel 23 at 12:00 P.M.
   Will she see all of the movie?

   _____

5. Write a problem using information
   from the schedule.

MIXED REVIEW

You can count the minutes by fives.

Write the time.

1.

2.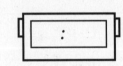

3.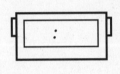

4.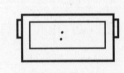

5.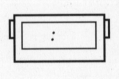

6.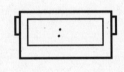

7.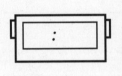

8.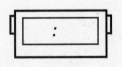

9.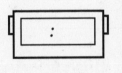

10.

McGraw-Hill School Division

MORE MENTAL MATH

Complete the problems.
Use mental math to solve.

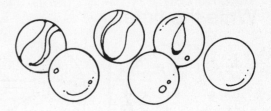

1. There are __6__ marbles.

   __4__ roll away.
   How many marbles are left?   __2__ marbles

   What if there are __60__ marbles

   and __40__ roll away?
   How many marbles are left?   __20__ marbles

2. There are _____ black checkers.

   There are _____ red checkers.
   How many checkers in all?   _____ checkers

   What if there are _____ black checkers

   and _____ red checkers?
   How many checkers in all?   _____ checkers

Add or subtract.

3. $9 - 2 =$ __7__ $6 + 2 =$ _____ $3 + 3 =$ _____

   $90 - 20 =$ __70__ $60 + 20 =$ _____ $30 + 30 =$ _____

4. $7 - 4 =$ _____ $5 - 3 =$ _____ $7 + 2 =$ _____

   $70 - 40 =$ _____ $50 - 30 =$ _____ $70 + 20 =$ _____

McGraw-Hill School Division

MIXED REVIEW

Write the time.

1.

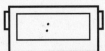

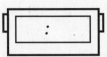

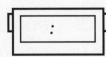

2.

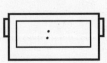

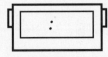

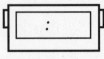

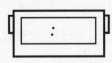

3.

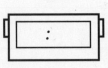

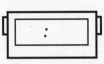

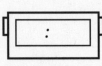

4.

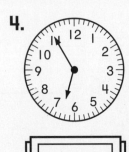

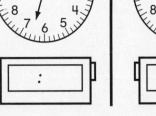

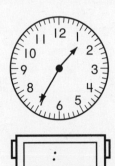

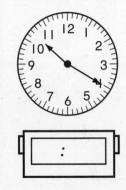

Name: _____

COUNT BACK BY TENS

Solve.

You can count back by tens.

1. 59 people were on the boat.
20 people got off to go swimming.
How many people are left on the boat? ___*39*___ people

2. 38 people were on the boat.
10 people left to see the fireworks.
How many people are still on the boat? _____ people

3. The boat holds 62 people.
There are 30 people on the boat.
How many more people can the boat hold? _____ people

Subtract.

4. 92 − 20 = ___*72*___   **5.** 85 − 30 = _____

6. 43 − 10 = _____   **7.** 65 − 20 = _____

8. 78 − 10 = _____   **9.** 56 − 30 = _____

10. 32 − 20 = _____   **11.** 97 − 20 = _____

12. 28 − 10 = _____   **13.** 74 − 30 = _____

14. 46 − 20 = _____   **15.** 81 − 20 = _____

16. 67 − 10 = _____   **17.** 72 − 30 = _____

18. 38 − 30 = _____   **19.** 59 − 10 = _____

MENTAL MATH

Solve.

Use mental math to count on or count back.

1. There were 84 children in line
   for the Ferris wheel.
   Then 3 more children got in line.
   How many children are in line now?   <u>87</u> children

2. Rita ordered 27 bags of peanuts.
   She counted 25 bags.
   How many bags of peanuts are missing?   _____ bags

3. The teacher had 43 tickets.
   Then she gave 2 tickets to Bob.
   How many tickets did she have left?   _____ tickets

4. 27 children were on the bumper cars.
   3 children got off the bumper cars.
   How many children are still on the cars?   _____ children

5. The popcorn man had 23 boxes.
   He sold 10 boxes of popcorn.
   How many boxes does he have now?   _____ boxes

6. There are 32 horses on the merry-go-round.
   There are 30 dragons.
   How many seats are on the
   merry-go-round?   _____ seats

Grade 2, Chapter 6, Lesson 2, Day 3, pages 211–212

McGraw-Hill School Division

PROBLEM-SOLVING STRATEGY: SOLVE 2-STEP PROBLEMS

Solve.

Show how you found the answer.

1. Sandy sold 28 rainbow ices.
He sold 10 lemon ices.
Then he sold 10 cherry ices.
How many ices did he sell in all?

__48__ ices

Step 1: __28 + 10 = 38__

Step 2: __38 + 10 = 48__

---

2. Tess made 41 sandwiches.
She sold 10 of them.
Then she made 3 more sandwiches.
How many does she have now?   _____ sandwiches

Step 1: _____   Step 2: _____

---

3. Mr. Washington bought 65 tickets.
He gave 20 tickets to his son.
He gave 30 tickets to his daughter.
How many tickets does Mr. Washington
have left?   _____ tickets

Step 1: _____   Step 2: _____

ADDITION STRATEGIES

Solve.
Use mental math.

1. Sam has 17 stamps from France.
Marie has 23 stamps from Spain.
How many stamps do they have
all together?   ___40___ stamps

2. Anna has 41 stamps from Mexico.
She has 34 stamps from Canada.
How many stamps does she have in all?   _____ stamps

3. Carl has stamps from 12 countries.
Alice has stamps from 15 different countries.
From how many countries do they both
have stamps?   _____ countries

4. Explain how you solved problem 3.

_____

_____

Add. Use mental math.

5. $49 + 11 =$ ___60___ $16 + 20 =$ _____ $72 + 27 =$ _____

6. $52 + 24 =$ _____ $38 + 9 =$ _____ $41 + 15 =$ _____

7. $21 + 44 =$ _____ $7 + 46 =$ _____ $66 + 13 =$ _____

8. $32 + 45 =$ _____ $25 + 25 =$ _____ $9 + 32 =$ _____

McGraw-Hill School Division

SUBTRACTION STRATEGIES

Solve.
Use mental math.

1. The shop had 56 rowboats to rent.
   16 people rented rowboats.
   How many rowboats are now in the shop? ___40___ rowboats

2. Louise had 34 baseballs in a bag.
   The team used 22 of them.
   How many baseballs are left in the bag? _____ baseballs

3. Kit spent $47 on a bike.
   He spent $16 on a helmet.
   How much more did he spend on the bike? $ _____

4. Explain how you solved problem 3.

   _____

   _____

Subtract.

5. $45 - 23 =$ __22__ $36 - 24 =$ _____ $86 - 14 =$ _____

6. $54 - 30 =$ _____ $75 - 15 =$ _____ $43 - 21 =$ _____

7. $66 - 12 =$ _____ $38 - 3 =$ _____ $29 - 10 =$ _____

8. $46 - 3 =$ _____ $59 - 11 =$ _____ $72 - 22 =$ _____

McGraw-Hill School Division

PROBLEM SOLVING: SOLVE MULTISTEP PROBLEMS

✔ Read
✔ Plan
✔ Solve
✔ Look Back

Solve.
Show your work.

1. Reggie put 20 streamers and 16 balloons
   around the yard.
   5 streamers and 4 balloons fell down.
   How many things are still up around
   the yard?   ___27___ things

   20 − 5 = 15; 16 − 4 = 12; 15 + 12 = 27

2. Shaun brought 25 cartons of juice to the party.
   Bill brought 13 cartons of juice.
   The people drank 10 cartons of apple juice
   and 8 cartons of grape juice.
   How many cartons of juice are left?   _____ cartons

3. Lois baked 48 muffins for the party.
   The children ate 20 orange muffins
   and 6 lemon muffins.
   Then some parents ate 3 more muffins.
   How many muffins are left?   _____ muffins

4. Write a word problem that
   uses addition and subtraction.

McGraw-Hill School Division

Name: _____

MIXED REVIEW

Count. Write how much money.

1.

64 ¢

2.

_____ ¢

3.

_____ ¢

4.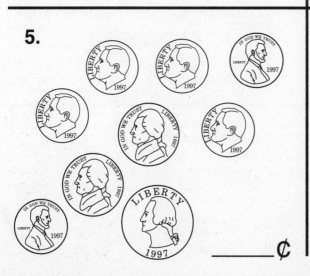

_____ ¢

5.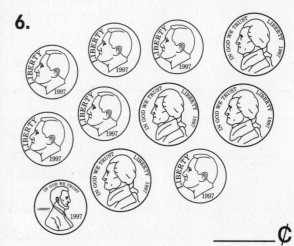

_____ ¢

6.

_____ ¢

MORE REGROUPING

Use ▭ and ◻.

Show the tens and ones.
Regroup when you can.
Write the number.

1. 1 ten, 13 ones

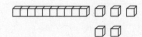

tens	ones
2	3

2. 1 ten, 5 ones

tens	ones

3. 2 tens, 10 ones

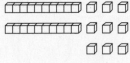

tens	ones

4. 1 ten, 19 ones

tens	ones

5. 1 ten, 11 ones

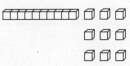

tens	ones

6. 2 tens, 18 ones

tens	ones

7. 1 ten, 14 ones

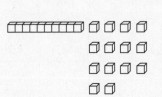

tens	ones

8. 4 tens, 2 ones

tens	ones

ADD 2-DIGIT NUMBERS

Add. Use tens and ones models to help.

1.

tens	ones
☐	
	6
+ 4	2
4	8

tens	ones
☐	
2	4
+ 1	6

tens	ones
☐	
1	9
+ 2	3

tens	ones
☐	
2	6
+	8

2.

tens	ones
☐	
3	4
+ 1	7

tens	ones
☐	
2	6
+ 3	3

tens	ones
☐	
4	5
+	9

tens	ones
☐	
5	1
+ 4	8

3.

tens	ones
☐	
6	5
+ 1	0

tens	ones
☐	
1	4
+ 2	8

tens	ones
☐	
5	3
+ 2	8

tens	ones
☐	
2	1
+ 2	8

MORE ADDING 2-DIGIT NUMBERS

Add.
Use tens and ones models to help.
Color the balloon if you regroup.

1.
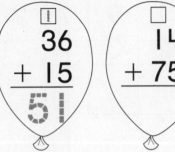

□ 1 □ □ □ □
36   14   19   47   28
+15 +75 +39 +36 +14
51

2.
□ □ □ □ □
  8   21   48   63   36
+49 +27 + 6 +24 +26

3.
□ □ □ □ □
13   56   17   15   49
+ 7 +29 +52 +18 +39

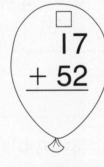

4.
□ □ □ □ □
25   43   39   38   57
+17 +26 +17 + 6 +17

McGraw-Hill School Division

ADD TO SOLVE PROBLEMS

Solve.

Workspace

1. Molly had 16 stickers.
She collected 22 more.
How many stickers does
Molly have now?   _38_

$$\begin{array}{r} 16 \\ + 22 \\ \hline 38 \end{array}$$

2. Dan read 9 books last month.
He read 15 books this month.
How many books did Dan read
during the two months?   _____

3. Tara made 25 paper planes.
Les made 37 paper planes.
How many planes did the two
children make in all?   _____

4. Write your own addition problem.
Solve it.

_____

_____

_____

PROBLEM-SOLVING STRATEGY: USE ESTIMATION

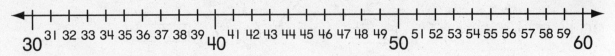

30 `31 32 33 34 35 36 37 38 39` 40 `41 42 43 44 45 46 47 48 49` 50 `51 52 53 54 55 56 57 58 59` 60

Solve. Use estimation.

1. Dana played two games of table tennis.
   She got a total of about 50 points.
   Which two scores are hers?

24   23   14

_____

2. José won two bags of marbles.
   He won about 80 marbles in all.
   Which two bags of marbles are his?

37   59   39

_____

3. Pat played ring toss two times.
   She got a total of about 70 points.
   Which two scores are hers?

59   23   44

_____

Grade 2, Chapter 7, Lesson 3, Day 1, pages 249–250

McGraw-Hill School Division

Name: _____

CHECK ADDITION

Add. Check your addition.
Then color to match the sum.

20 to 29 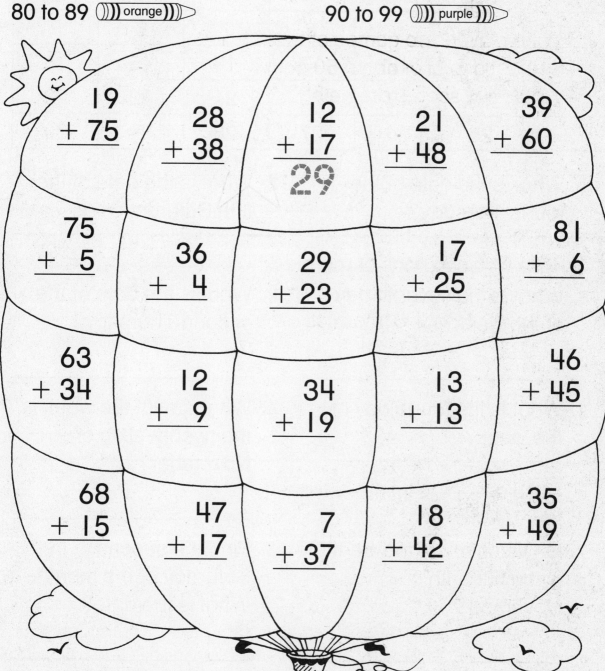 red
50 to 59 green
80 to 89 orange

40 to 49 blue
60 to 69 yellow
90 to 99 purple

19
+ 75

28
+ 38

12
+ 17
29

21
+ 48

39
+ 60

75
+ 5

36
+ 4

29
+ 23

17
+ 25

81
+ 6

63
+ 34

12
+ 9

34
+ 19

13
+ 13

46
+ 45

68
+ 15

47
+ 17

7
+ 37

18
+ 42

35
+ 49

McGraw-Hill School Division

MIXED REVIEW

Use the calendar to solve.

November						
Sun.	Mon.	Tues.	Wed.	Thurs.	Fri.	Sat.
					1	2
3	4	5	6	7	8	9
10	11	12	13	14	15	16
17	18	19	20	21	22	23
24	25	26	27	28	29	30

1. What is the date of the fourth Tuesday?

_____

2. What is the date of the fifth Saturday?

_____

3. What is the seventh day of the week?

_____

4. What is the date of the second Thursday?

_____

5. What is the fourth day of the week?

_____

6. What day of the week is the twenty-sixth of November?

_____

7. On what day of the week is the fifteenth of November?

_____

8. Find the second Saturday of the month. What is the date?

_____

MORE ADDING MONEY

Add.

1.
$$22\cent + 29\cent = \boxed{51}\cent$$

$$35\cent + 19\cent + 16\cent$$

$$15\cent + 19\cent + 39\cent$$

$$25\cent + 35\cent + 20\cent$$

2.
$$16\cent + 10\cent + 22\cent$$

$$25\cent + 29\cent + 12\cent$$

$$66\cent + 3\cent + 11\cent$$

$$24\cent + 31\cent + 35\cent$$

3.
$$29\cent + 55\cent$$

$$34\cent + 21\cent$$

$$75\cent + 24\cent$$

$$28\cent + 12\cent$$

4. What strategies did you use to add?

_____

_____

McGraw-Hill School Division

PROBLEM SOLVING: CHOOSE THE METHOD

Solve.
Choose the best method for you.

Workspace

1. Mario made 25 cards.
Later he made 13 more.
How many cards did
Mario make?   38

2. Liz used 59 beads for a
necklace. She used 27 beads
for a bracelet. How many
beads did Liz use?   _____

3. Margo planted 20 seeds in
the morning. Later, she
planted 30 more seeds. How
many seeds did Margo plant?   _____

4. Steve blew up balloons for
his party. He blew up 19
red balloons, 26 blue
balloons, and 37 yellow
balloons. How many
balloons did Steve blow up?   _____

McGraw-Hill School Division

MIXED REVIEW

Add. Did you regroup?

1.
   □   □   □

  32   (Yes)   57   Yes   63   Yes

+ 29   No   + 38   No   + 6   No

  61

2.
   □   □   □

  14   Yes   8   Yes   46   Yes

+ 85   No   + 72   No   + 37   No

Add.

3.

12	18	20	5	33	26
+ 19	+ 59	+ 61	+ 32	+ 55	+ 32

4.

22	34	15	75	49	52
+ 17	+ 27	+ 18	+ 9	+ 49	+ 21

5.

36	46	4	23	27	65
+ 24	+ 40	+ 20	+ 14	+ 27	+ 34

Name: _____

MORE REGROUPING

Use 5 ▭▭▭ and 10 ▢.
Complete the chart.

	Show.	Take away.	Did you regroup?		Number left.
1.	24	11	yes	(no)	13
2.	45	37	yes	no	
3.	33	9	yes	no	
4.	51	26	yes	no	
5.	46	25	yes	no	
6.	19	12	yes	no	
7.	38	19	yes	no	
8.	52	34	yes	no	
9.	27	7	yes	no	
10.	56	18	yes	no	

Grade 2, Chapter 8, Lesson 1, Day 2, pages 277–278

McGraw-Hill School Division

SUBTRACT 2-DIGIT NUMBERS

Subtract. Use tens and ones models to help.

1.

tens	ones
[2]	[grid]
3	4
1	6
1	8

tens	ones
□	□
4	9
2	3
2	6

tens	ones
[5]	□
6	15
3	7
2	8

tens	ones
[4]	□
5	11
1	8
3	3

2.

tens	ones
[6]	□
7	13
2	9
4	4

tens	ones
[7]	□
8	12
1	7
6	5

tens	ones
[8]	□
9	10
3	4
5	6

tens	ones
[1]	□
2	18
	9
1	8

3.

tens	ones
□	□
3	6
1	4
2	2

tens	ones
[4]	□
5	14
2	5
2	9

tens	ones
[5]	□
6	13
3	6
2	7

tens	ones
[6]	□
7	17
1	9
5	6

MORE SUBTRACTING 2-DIGIT NUMBERS

Subtract. Use tens and ones models to help.

1.
$$\begin{array}{r} 2\ 12 \\ \cancel{3}2 \\ -17 \\ \hline 15 \end{array}$$
$$\begin{array}{r} 58 \\ -29 \\ \hline 31 \end{array}$$
$$\begin{array}{r} 45 \\ -16 \\ \hline 31 \end{array}$$
$$\begin{array}{r} 76 \\ -34 \\ \hline 42 \end{array}$$
$$\begin{array}{r} 61 \\ -25 \\ \hline 36 \end{array}$$
$$\begin{array}{r} 83 \\ -48 \\ \hline 45 \end{array}$$

2.
$$\begin{array}{r} 94 \\ -55 \\ \hline 41 \end{array}$$
$$\begin{array}{r} 60 \\ -23 \\ \hline 43 \end{array}$$
$$\begin{array}{r} 21 \\ -8 \\ \hline 27 \end{array}$$
$$\begin{array}{r} 56 \\ -37 \\ \hline 21 \end{array}$$
$$\begin{array}{r} 43 \\ -15 \\ \hline 32 \end{array}$$
$$\begin{array}{r} 72 \\ -36 \\ \hline 44 \end{array}$$

3.
$$\begin{array}{r} 38 \\ -14 \\ \hline 24 \end{array}$$
$$\begin{array}{r} 85 \\ -28 \\ \hline 63 \end{array}$$
$$\begin{array}{r} 64 \\ -39 \\ \hline 35 \end{array}$$
$$\begin{array}{r} 70 \\ -41 \\ \hline 31 \end{array}$$
$$\begin{array}{r} 99 \\ -57 \\ \hline 42 \end{array}$$
$$\begin{array}{r} 51 \\ -22 \\ \hline 31 \end{array}$$

4.
$$\begin{array}{r} 27 \\ -9 \\ \hline 22 \end{array}$$
$$\begin{array}{r} 42 \\ -13 \\ \hline 31 \end{array}$$
$$\begin{array}{r} 56 \\ -24 \\ \hline 32 \end{array}$$
$$\begin{array}{r} 63 \\ -30 \\ \hline 33 \end{array}$$
$$\begin{array}{r} 88 \\ -49 \\ \hline 41 \end{array}$$
$$\begin{array}{r} 74 \\ -55 \\ \hline 21 \end{array}$$

5.
$$\begin{array}{r} 91 \\ -38 \\ \hline 67 \end{array}$$
$$\begin{array}{r} 37 \\ -16 \\ \hline 41 \end{array}$$
$$\begin{array}{r} 75 \\ -27 \\ \hline 56 \end{array}$$
$$\begin{array}{r} 50 \\ -18 \\ \hline 48 \end{array}$$
$$\begin{array}{r} 62 \\ -26 \\ \hline 44 \end{array}$$
$$\begin{array}{r} 49 \\ -32 \\ \hline 16 \end{array}$$

SUBTRACT TO SOLVE PROBLEMS

Lion
43 inches

Moose
66 inches

Yak
72 inches

Gazelle
34 inches

You can subtract to **compare.**
Solve.

Workspace

1. Which animal is taller,
   the lion or the yak?   ___yak___

   How much taller?   _____ inches

$$\begin{array}{r} {}^{6}\;{}^{12} \\ \not7\not2 \\ -\,43 \\ \hline 29 \end{array}$$

2. How much taller is the
   yak than the moose?   _____ inches

3. Which animal is shorter,
   the gazelle or the moose?   _____

   How much shorter?   _____ inches

4. How much shorter is the
   lion than the moose?   _____ inches

PROBLEM-SOLVING
STRATEGY: MAKE A LIST

Make a list to show all the two-digit numbers.

1. A scientist tags sea turtles.
   She uses the numbers 1, 5, and 7
   to make two-digit tag numbers.
   What numbers can she make? _____

2. Dr. Brown made tags for some swans.
   What two-digit numbers can
   she make with 1, 3, and 8? _____

3. Dr. Stone tags bull sharks in the sea.
   He uses the numbers 4, 7, and 9
   to make two-digit tag numbers.
   What numbers can he make? _____

4. Dr. Lane tags wolf pups.
   He uses the numbers 1, 3, 5,
   and 7 to make two-digit numbers.
   What numbers can he make?

   _____

5. A group of scientists tags zebras.
   The scientists use the numbers 2, 4,
   6, and 9 to make two-digit numbers.
   What numbers can they make?

   _____

MIXED REVIEW

Add.

1.
   12¢   73¢   57¢   35¢   49¢
+ 46¢   + 18¢   + 31¢   + 8¢   + 22¢

   58¢

2.
   27¢   84¢   9¢   63¢   5¢
+ 9¢   + 13¢   + 18¢   + 36¢   + 90¢

3.
   56¢   72¢   14¢   38¢   41¢
+ 7¢   + 19¢   + 35¢   + 38¢   + 7¢

4.
   82¢   6¢   28¢   91¢   67¢
+ 15¢   + 24¢   + 32¢   + 7¢   + 22¢

5.
   15¢   21¢   8¢   70¢   62¢
    2¢   14¢   37¢   9¢   23¢
+ 48¢   + 53¢   + 33¢   + 19¢   + 14¢

6.
   50¢   4¢   38¢   25¢   47¢
   17¢   29¢   1¢   11¢   46¢
+ 12¢   + 53¢   + 17¢   + 30¢   + 4¢

CHECK SUBTRACTION

Subtract. Then add to check the difference.

1.
$$\begin{array}{r} {}^{4\ 13} \\ \cancel{53} \\ -25 \\ \hline 28 \end{array}$$
$$\begin{array}{r} 28 \\ +25 \\ \hline 53 \end{array}$$
$$\begin{array}{r} 49¢ \\ -16¢ \\ \hline \end{array}$$
$$\begin{array}{r} 85 \\ -37 \\ \hline \end{array}$$

2.
$$\begin{array}{r} 62¢ \\ -41¢ \\ \hline \end{array}$$
$$\begin{array}{r} 90 \\ -55 \\ \hline \end{array}$$
$$\begin{array}{r} 74¢ \\ -39¢ \\ \hline \end{array}$$

3.
$$\begin{array}{r} 37 \\ -\ 8 \\ \hline \end{array}$$
$$\begin{array}{r} \$82 \\ -\$14 \\ \hline \end{array}$$
$$\begin{array}{r} 59 \\ -22 \\ \hline \end{array}$$

4.
$$\begin{array}{r} 73 \\ -29 \\ \hline \end{array}$$
$$\begin{array}{r} 56 \\ -20 \\ \hline \end{array}$$
$$\begin{array}{r} \$61 \\ -\$58 \\ \hline \end{array}$$

Solve. Then add to check your answers.   Workspace

5. The class counted 43 ducks flying. They counted 16 ducks swimming. How many more ducks were flying than swimming? _____

6. Joy counted 27 of the 43 ducks. How many of the ducks did Joy *not* count? _____

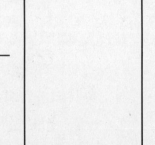

McGraw-Hill School Division

Grade 2, Chapter 8, Lesson 5, Day 1, pages 297–298

ADD OR SUBTRACT TO SOLVE PROBLEMS

Add or subtract to solve.   Workspace

1. There are 41 zebras eating grass. There are 26 zebras drinking water. How many more zebras are eating than drinking? _____

2. One zoo ticket costs $8. How much will two zoo tickets cost? _____

3. Mrs. Miller had $51. She spent $32 on zoo tickets. How much money does she have left? _____

4. Mr. Lucas wants to buy a camera that costs $24. He has $11. How much more money does he need? _____

5. Write your own word problem. Use the numbers 60 and 47. Have a partner solve it.

PROBLEM SOLVING: IDENTIFY EXTRA INFORMATION

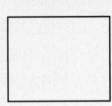

✔ Read
✔ Plan
✔ Solve
✔ Look Back

Cross out any extra information.
Then solve.

Workspace

1. A gray whale is about 39 feet long.
A finback whale is about 82 feet long.
A right whale is about 55 feet long.
How much longer is the right
whale than the gray whale?

_____ feet

2. A whale went underwater for 30 minutes.
She came up for 10 minutes.
Then she went underwater for 45 minutes.
How many minutes was she underwater in all?

<u> 85 </u> minutes

What should the answer be?   _____ minutes

3. How could someone get 85 as the answer?
Write about it.

_____

_____

4. Write a problem with extra information.
Have a partner solve it.

MIXED REVIEW

Solve.

1. Rita picked 38 pounds of peaches one morning. The next morning she picked 20 more pounds. How many pounds did she pick in 2 mornings?

You can count by tens: 38, 48, 58.

_58_ pounds

2. 75 pounds of peaches were taken to a store. The store already had 10 pounds of peaches. How many pounds of peaches were at the store?

_____ pounds

3. On Tuesday, James and his uncle canned 13 pounds of peaches. On Saturday, they canned 30 more pounds of peaches. How many pounds of peaches did they can altogether?

_____ pounds

Add.

4. $47 + 10 =$ _____

5. $58 + 30 =$ _____

6. $66 + 20 =$ _____

7. $12 + 10 =$ _____

8. $81 + 10 =$ _____

9. $73 + 20 =$ _____

THREE-DIMENSIONAL SHAPES

1   2   3   4   5

Find the shapes in the picture.
Write the number of the shape on the object.

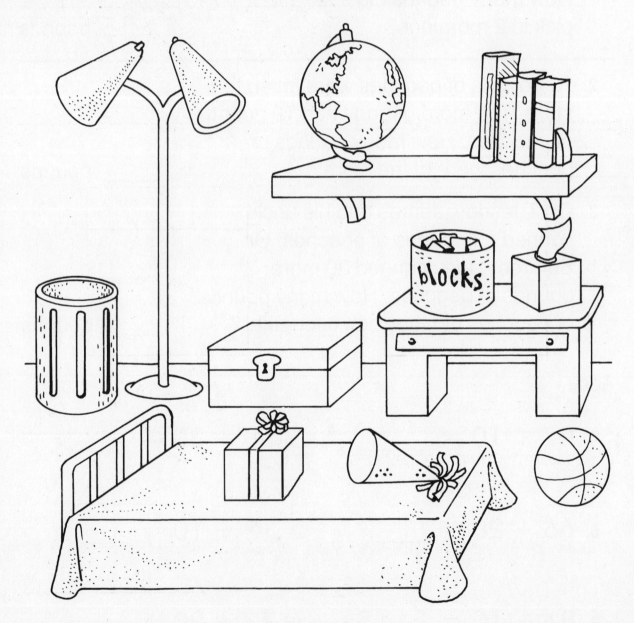

blocks

McGraw-Hill School Division

TWO-DIMENSIONAL SHAPES

How many squares are in these rectangles?

1.

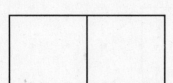

2.

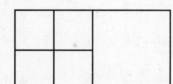

3.

_2_ _____   _____   _____

How many rectangles are in these squares?

4.

5.

_____   _____

6. How many squares are
in this triangle?   _____

7. How many triangles?   _____

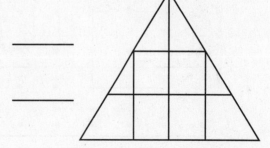

CONGRUENT SHAPES

Draw a rectangle that is congruent.

1.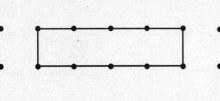

2.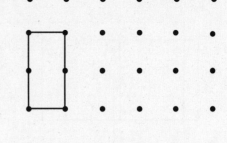

Draw a triangle that is congruent.

3.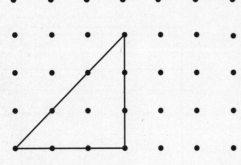

4.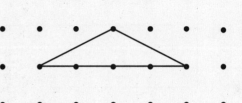

Draw a square that is congruent.

5.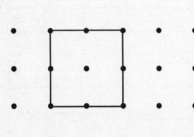

6.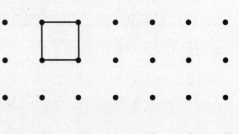

McGraw-Hill School Division

Name: _____

SYMMETRY

Make a shape using the line of symmetry.
Draw the matching part.

1.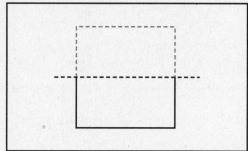

2.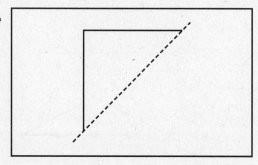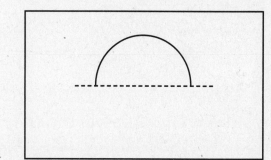

3.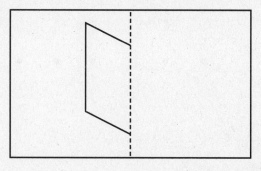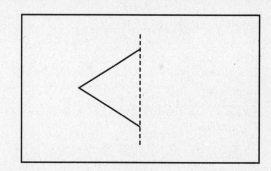

4.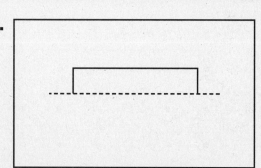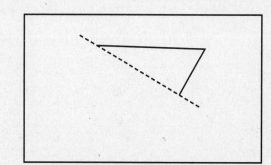

PROBLEM-SOLVING STRATEGY: USE A PATTERN

Draw to complete each pattern.
Then count the shapes.

1. Timothy is making a book mark. There will be 19 shapes in the pattern. How many triangles will he make?

16 triangles

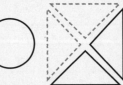

2. Kim makes a chalk drawing on a wall. She will make 21 shapes in her drawing. How many diamonds will she make?

_____

3. Lyn draws a rectangle around 2 small circles. There are 14 circles in her pattern. How many rectangles will she draw?

_____

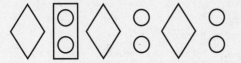

MIXED REVIEW

Subtract. Use tens and ones models to help.

1. $\begin{array}{r} \cancel{7}\cancel{6} \\ -19 \\ \hline 57 \end{array}$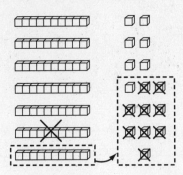

2. $\begin{array}{r} 35 \\ -11 \\ \hline \end{array}$

3.

$\begin{array}{r} 26 \\ -7 \\ \hline \end{array}$ $\begin{array}{r} 88 \\ -39 \\ \hline \end{array}$ $\begin{array}{r} 72 \\ -51 \\ \hline \end{array}$ $\begin{array}{r} 36 \\ -18 \\ \hline \end{array}$ $\begin{array}{r} 31 \\ -10 \\ \hline \end{array}$ $\begin{array}{r} 44 \\ -9 \\ \hline \end{array}$

4.

$\begin{array}{r} 20 \\ -12 \\ \hline \end{array}$ $\begin{array}{r} 65 \\ -54 \\ \hline \end{array}$ $\begin{array}{r} 61 \\ -29 \\ \hline \end{array}$ $\begin{array}{r} 50 \\ -47 \\ \hline \end{array}$ $\begin{array}{r} 25 \\ -15 \\ \hline \end{array}$ $\begin{array}{r} 95 \\ -36 \\ \hline \end{array}$

Solve.

5. How many more square kites than diamond-shaped kites?

Kite-Flying Contest	
Square kites	27
Diamond-shaped kites	8

Workspace

There are _____ more square kites.

FRACTIONS

Write the fraction for the shaded part.

1.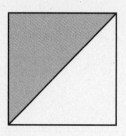

2.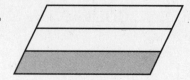

3.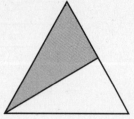

4.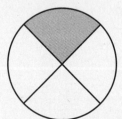

5.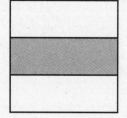

6.

7.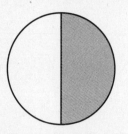

8.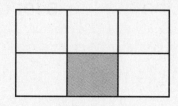

9.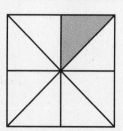

10.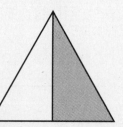

Grade 2, Chapter 9, Lesson 6, Day 1, pages 331–332

MORE FRACTIONS

Write the fraction for the part that is left.

1. $\frac{2}{4}$ of the sandwich is for Jesse.

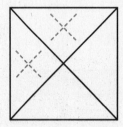

How much is left? $\frac{2}{4}$

2. $\frac{3}{5}$ of the juice is for April.

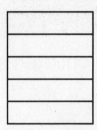

How much is left? _____

3. $\frac{3}{6}$ of the pie is for Nina.

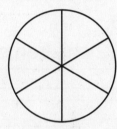

How much is left? _____

4. $\frac{2}{3}$ of the orange is for Daniel.

How much is left? _____

5. Write a problem about sharing a watermelon.

_____

_____

McGraw-Hill School Division

FRACTION OF A GROUP

Color the part that each child gets.
Write the fraction that each child gets.

1. 4 children share equally.

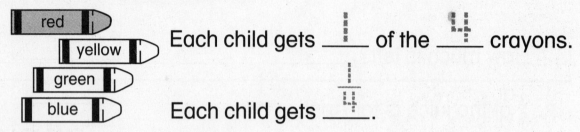

Each child gets ___ 1 ___ of the ___ 4 ___ crayons.

Each child gets ___ 1/4 ___ .

2. 3 children share equally.

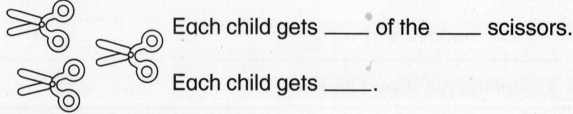

Each child gets _____ of the _____ scissors.

Each child gets _____ .

3. 2 children share equally.

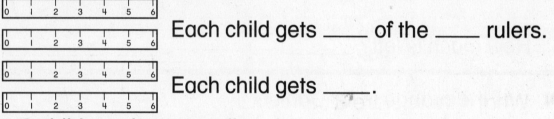

Each child gets _____ of the _____ rulers.

Each child gets _____ .

4. 2 children share equally.

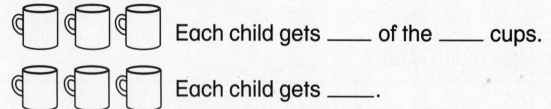

Each child gets _____ of the _____ cups.

Each child gets _____ .

5. 4 children share equally.

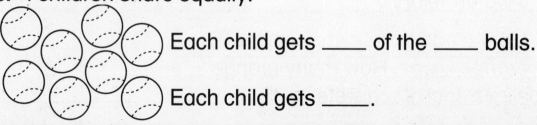

Each child gets _____ of the _____ balls.

Each child gets _____ .

McGraw-Hill School Division

PROBLEM SOLVING: DRAW A PICTURE

✔ Read
✔ Plan
✔ Solve
✔ Look Back

Draw a picture to solve.

Use your own paper.

1. Tanya and 2 friends share 3 apples. How many apples does each child get?

   l apple

2. Robert and a friend share a box of 6 crayons. How many crayons does each child get?

   _____

3. Lea and her brother share a bag of 10 marbles. How many marbles does each child get?

   _____

4. What if there were 8 marbles in the box? How many marbles would Lea and her brother get?

   _____

5. Evan and 3 friends share 12 pieces of drawing paper. How many pieces of paper does each child get?

   _____

6. Mariko and her 2 sisters share 9 orange slices. How many orange slices does each sister get?

   _____

MIXED REVIEW

Add. Use tens and ones models to help.

1. ☐
$$\begin{array}{r} 19 \\ +\ 34 \\ \hline 53 \end{array}$$

2. ☐
$$\begin{array}{r} 21 \\ +\ 25 \\ \hline 46 \end{array}$$

3.

☐	☐	☐	☐	☐	☐
$\begin{array}{r}14\\+26\\\hline\end{array}$	$\begin{array}{r}35\\+41\\\hline\end{array}$	$\begin{array}{r}87\\+\ 5\\\hline\end{array}$	$\begin{array}{r}11\\+59\\\hline\end{array}$	$\begin{array}{r}44\\+22\\\hline\end{array}$	$\begin{array}{r}8\\+51\\\hline\end{array}$

4.

☐	☐	☐	☐	☐	☐
$\begin{array}{r}21\\+21\\\hline\end{array}$	$\begin{array}{r}89\\+\ 7\\\hline\end{array}$	$\begin{array}{r}54\\+17\\\hline\end{array}$	$\begin{array}{r}61\\+18\\\hline\end{array}$	$\begin{array}{r}72\\+\ 9\\\hline\end{array}$	$\begin{array}{r}35\\+28\\\hline\end{array}$

5.

☐	☐	☐	☐	☐	☐
$\begin{array}{r}66\\+19\\\hline\end{array}$	$\begin{array}{r}15\\+29\\\hline\end{array}$	$\begin{array}{r}33\\+24\\\hline\end{array}$	$\begin{array}{r}9\\+11\\\hline\end{array}$	$\begin{array}{r}2\\+37\\\hline\end{array}$	$\begin{array}{r}74\\+16\\\hline\end{array}$

6.

☐	☐	☐	☐	☐	☐
$\begin{array}{r}25\\+25\\\hline\end{array}$	$\begin{array}{r}48\\+26\\\hline\end{array}$	$\begin{array}{r}59\\+\ 9\\\hline\end{array}$	$\begin{array}{r}7\\+14\\\hline\end{array}$	$\begin{array}{r}68\\+18\\\hline\end{array}$	$\begin{array}{r}92\\+\ 4\\\hline\end{array}$

Inch and Foot

Use a [ruler] to measure each path.

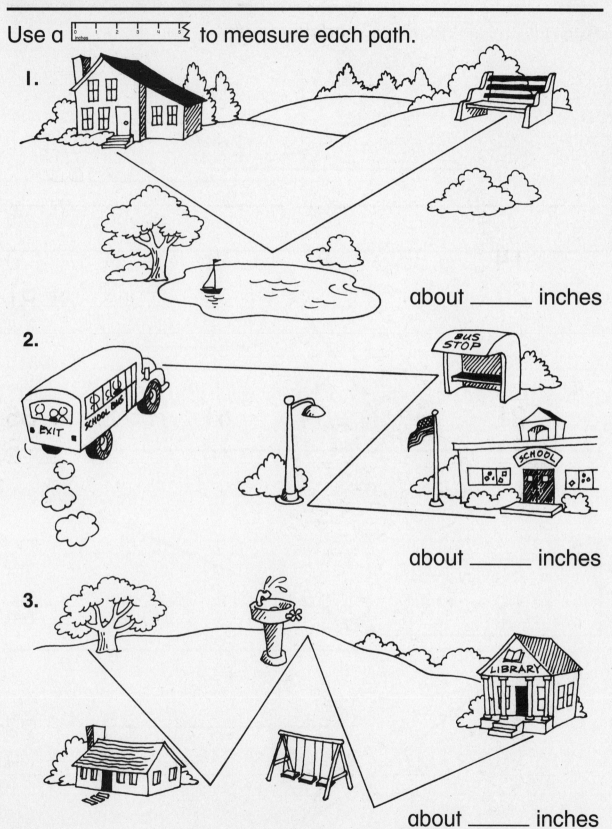

1.

about _____ inches

2.

about _____ inches

3.

about _____ inches

McGraw-Hill School Division

CENTIMETER

Use a [ruler] to measure the 🚗 path.

1.

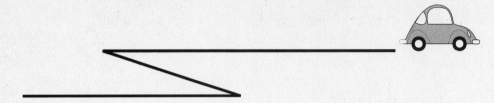

about ⌐8⌐ cm

2.

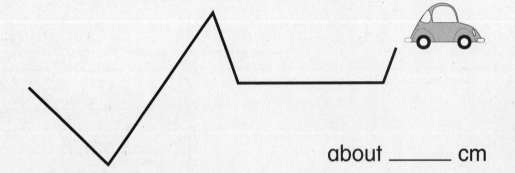

about _____ cm

3.

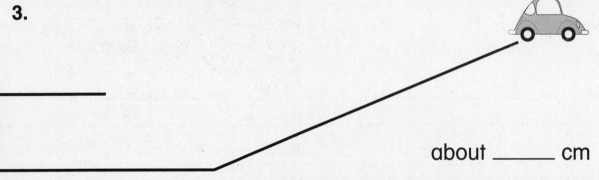

about _____ cm

4.

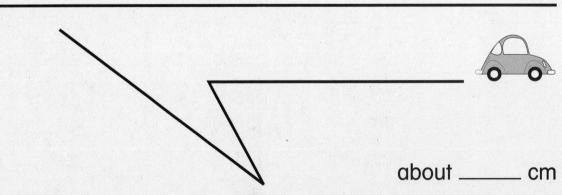

about _____ cm

PERIMETER

Measure. Add to find the perimeter.

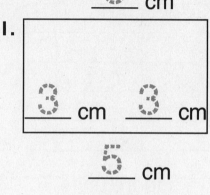

1.

_5_ cm

_3_ cm   _3_ cm

_5_ cm

_16_ cm

2.

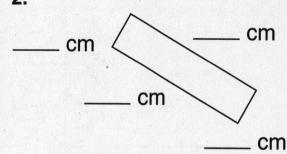

____ cm   ____ cm

____ cm

____ cm

____ cm

3.

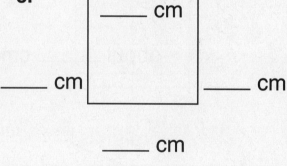

____ cm

____ cm   ____ cm

____ cm

____ cm

4.

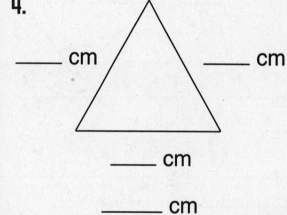

____ cm   ____ cm

____ cm

____ cm

5.

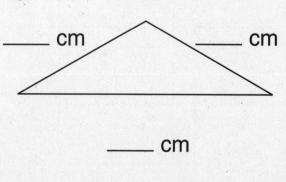

____ cm   ____ cm

____ cm

____ cm

6.

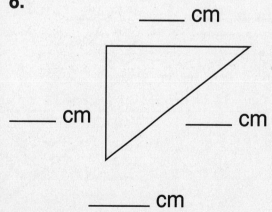

____ cm

____ cm   ____ cm

____ cm

AREA

Color to show the number of square units.

1.

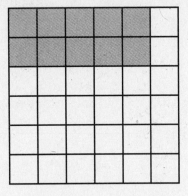

10 square units

2.

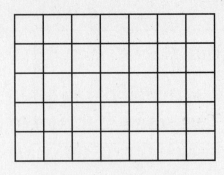

14 square units

3.

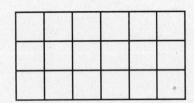

15 square units

4.

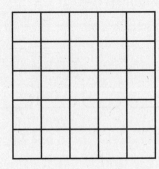

16 square units

Color the area.
Write how many square units you colored.

5.

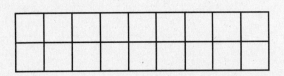

_____ square units

6.

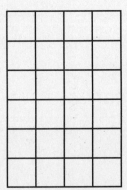

_____ square units

PROBLEM-SOLVING STRATEGY: DRAW A DIAGRAM

Draw a diagram to solve.

1. Kim put  around a .

   Two sides of the table have 5 chairs.
   Two sides of the table have 2 chairs.
   How many chairs did Kim use?

   _____ chairs

2.

   Marty puts cards on the table.
   He puts 4 cards in a row.
   He makes 4 rows.
   How many cards does he use?

   _____ cards

3. Cars are parked in a lot.
   There are 3 rows.
   7 cars are parked in each row.
   How many cars are parked in
   the lot?

   _____ cars

POUND

Write *more than* or *less than*.

1.

less than I pound

2.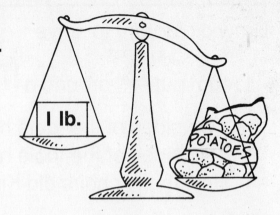

_____ I pound

3.

_____ I pound

4.

_____ I pound

How many pounds?

5.

about _____ pounds

6.

about _____ pounds

KILOGRAM

Write *more than* or *less than*.

kg means
kilogram.

1.

<u>**more than**</u> I kilogram

2.

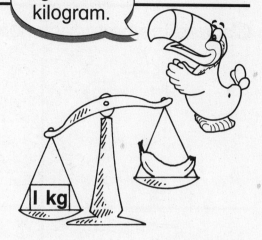

_____ I kilogram

3.

_____ I kilogram

4.

_____ I kilogram

How many kilograms?

5.

about _____ kilograms

6.

about _____ kilograms

Name:

CUP, PINT, QUART

Choose the better estimate.

1.	 cup	 (more than 1 cup) less than 1 cup
2.	 quart	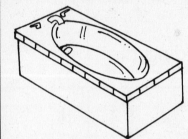 more than 1 quart less than 1 quart
3.	pint	 more than 1 pint less than 1 pint
4.	pint	 more than 1 pint less than 1 pint
5.	cup	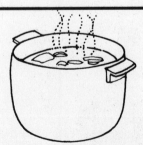 more than 1 cup less than 1 cup

Grade 2, Chapter 10, Lesson 5, Day 1, pages 371–372

McGraw-Hill School Division

Name: _____

LITER

Choose the better estimate.

1.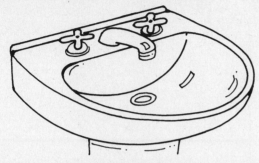

more than 1 liter

less than 1 liter

2.

more than 1 liter

less than 1 liter

3.

more than 1 liter

less than 1 liter

4.

more than 1 liter

less than 1 liter

5.

more than 1 liter

less than 1 liter

McGraw-Hill School Division

MIXED REVIEW

Write the fraction for the shaded part.

1.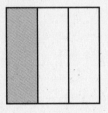

2.

3.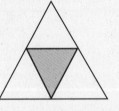

4.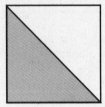

5.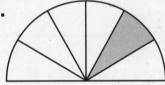

6.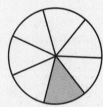

7.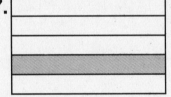

8.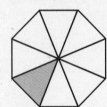

9.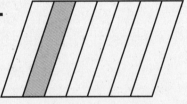

10.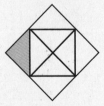

11.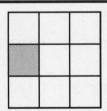

12.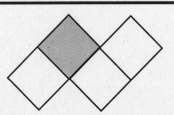

Grade 2, Chapter 10, Lesson 6, Day 1, pages 375–376

MEASUREMENT TOOLS

Match to show which tool you would use to measure.

1.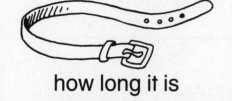
how much it holds

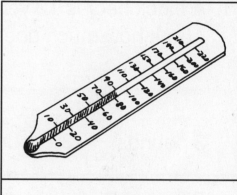

2.
how long it is

3.
how hot it is

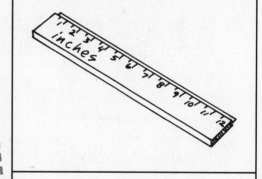

4.
how heavy it is

5.
how much it weighs

6.
how much it holds

McGraw-Hill School Division

PROBLEM SOLVING: FIND REASONABLE ANSWERS

✔ Read
✔ Plan
✔ Solve
✔ Look Back

Ring the answer that makes sense.

1. A black bear is 12 years old.
   About how much does she weigh?

   3 pounds   30 pounds   (300 pounds)

2. Billy and Diana play catch.
   About how far apart do they stand?

   I foot   15 feet   50 feet

3. Ricky gives his baby brother a bottle of milk.
   About how much milk does the baby drink?

   I cup   2 pints   3 quarts

4. Ann Marie is ice skating.
   About what temperature is it?

   25°F   52°F   95°F

McGraw-Hill School Division

MIXED REVIEW

Measure.
Add to find the perimeter.

1.

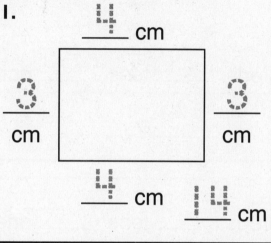

2.

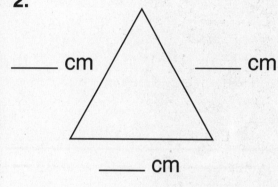

3.

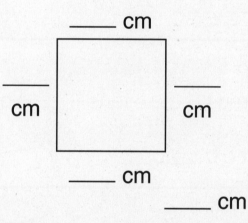

4.

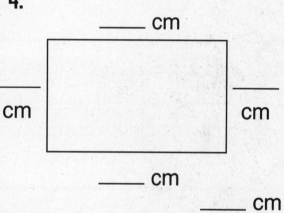

5.

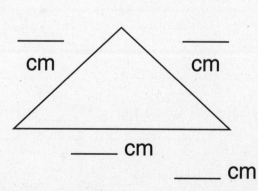

6.

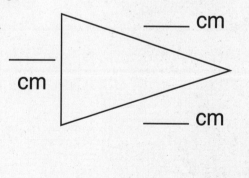

McGraw-Hill School Division

HUNDREDS, TENS, AND ONES

Write how many hundreds, tens, and ones.
Write the number.

I.  __2__ hundreds __5__ tens __3__ ones

__253__

2. ____ hundreds ____ tens ____ ones

_____

3. 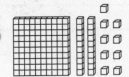 ____ hundreds ____ tens ____ ones

_____

4. 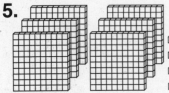 ____ hundreds ____ tens ____ ones

_____

5. ____ hundreds ____ tens ____ ones

_____

Grade 2, Chapter 11, Lesson 1, Day 2, pages 393–394

McGraw-Hill School Division

Name: _____

PLACE VALUE

Write how many hundreds, tens, and ones.
Write the number.

1.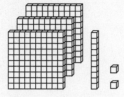

hundreds	tens	ones
3	1	2	312

2.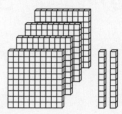

hundreds	tens	ones
			___

3.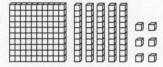

hundreds	tens	ones
			___

4.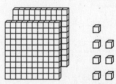

hundreds	tens	ones
			___

5.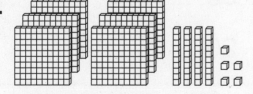

hundreds	tens	ones
			___

6.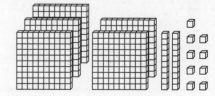

hundreds	tens	ones
			___

VALUE OF A DIGIT

Circle to show the value of the underlined digit.

1. 2<u>3</u>5	300	(30)	3
2. 67<u>9</u>	900	90	9
3. <u>8</u>25	800	80	8
4. <u>1</u>43	100	10	1
5. 6<u>5</u>	500	50	5
6. 7<u>9</u>2	900	90	9
7. <u>3</u>47	300	30	3
8. 42<u>6</u>	600	60	6
9. 5<u>1</u>2	100	10	1
10. <u>9</u>71	900	90	9
11. <u>6</u>0	600	60	6
12. 2<u>2</u>2	200	20	2
13. <u>6</u>86	600	60	6
14. 40<u>3</u>	300	30	3
15. <u>5</u>62	500	50	5

Grade 2, Chapter 11, Lesson 2, Day 2, pages 397–398

McGraw-Hill School Division

ORDER TO 1,000

Write the missing numbers.

1. 321, 322, <u>323</u>, <u>324</u>, 325, <u>326</u>, <u>327</u>

2. 753, 754, ____, ____, 757, 758, ____

3. 471, ____, ____, ____, 475, ____, 477

4. 987, 988, ____, ____, ____, 992, ____

5. 217, ____, ____, 220, ____, 222, ____

6. 538, 537, ____, ____, 534, ____, 532

7. 875, 874, ____, ____, 871, ____, ____

8. 662, ____, ____, ____, 666, 667, ____

9. 140, 141, ____, ____, ____, ____, ____

10. ____, 773, 774, ____, ____, ____, ____

11. 499, 498, ____, ____, 495, ____, ____

12. ____, 661, 662, ____, ____, 665, ____

BEFORE, AFTER, BETWEEN

Write the number just after, just before,
or between.

1. | 233 | 234 | 403 | | | | 998 |

2. | 665 | | 667 | | 123 | |

3. | 590 | | 777 | | | | 321 |

4. | 892 | | 894 | | 107 | | 109 |

5. | | 438 | 699 | | 701 |

6. | 324 | | 326 | | 591 | | 593 |

7. | | 276 | 433 | | 761 | |

8. | 229 | | 231 | | | 804 |

COMPARE NUMBERS TO 1,000

Compare. Write < or >.

1. 276 ⊘> 176   214 ◯ 219   582 ◯ 526

2. 653 ◯ 673   419 ◯ 429   137 ◯ 132

3. 350 ◯ 250   79 ◯ 109   533 ◯ 543

4. 738 ◯ 718   652 ◯ 526   920 ◯ 925

5. 254 ◯ 244   679 ◯ 678   302 ◯ 320

6. 891 ◯ 890   919 ◯ 929   656 ◯ 556

7. 445 ◯ 440   331 ◯ 338   710 ◯ 712

8. 179 ◯ 189   216 ◯ 116   379 ◯ 279

9. 89 ◯ 119   772 ◯ 771   542 ◯ 245

10. 319 ◯ 317   570 ◯ 470   619 ◯ 639

11. 112 ◯ 109   981 ◯ 918   425 ◯ 335

12. 299 ◯ 298   603 ◯ 630   181 ◯ 191

REGROUPING FOR ADDITION

Use models. Show the hundreds, tens,
and ones. Regroup when you can.
Write the number.

1. 2 hundreds 12 tens
4 ones

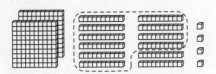

hundreds	tens	ones
3	2	4

2. 5 hundreds 4 tens
7 ones

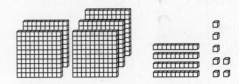

hundreds	tens	ones

3. 6 hundreds 16 tens

hundreds	tens	ones

4. 2 hundreds 13 tens
5 ones

hundreds	tens	ones

5. 4 hundreds 8 tens 4 ones

hundreds	tens	ones

6. 3 hundreds 14 tens
8 ones

hundreds	tens	ones

Grade 2, Chapter 11, Lesson 4, Day 1, pages 413–414

ADD 3-DIGIT NUMBERS

Add. Use hundreds, tens, and ones models
to help.

1.

hundreds	tens	ones
□ 4	□ 1	9
+ 3	6	5
7	8	4

hundreds	tens	ones
□ 2	□ 7	3
+ 1	6	5

2.

hundreds	tens	ones
□	□ 6	1
+ 3	7	4

hundreds	tens	ones
□ 6	□ 3	7
+ 2	2	5

3.

hundreds	tens	ones
□ 4	□ 3	8
+		7

hundreds	tens	ones
□ 2	□ 6	9
+ 3	5	0

MORE ADDING 3-DIGIT NUMBERS

Add.

1.

☐☐	☐☐	☐	☐☐	☐☐
153	67	460	327	548
+378	+258	+254	+175	+ 93
531				

2.

☐		☐☐	☐☐	☐
186	735	655	347	6
+241	+264	+ 75	+278	+465

3.

☐	☐☐	☐☐	☐☐	
452	573	294	695	708
+ 70	+378	+267	+ 8	+141

Solve.   Workspace

4. 279 people came to the concert on
Saturday. 356 people came to the
concert on Sunday. How many people
came to the concert on both days?

_____ people

5. Write a word problem.
Use the numbers 365 and 578.
Then solve the problem.

REGROUPING FOR SUBTRACTION

Use ▦ , ▭ , and ◻ to show the number.
Complete the chart.

	Show.	Take away.	Did you regroup?		Number left
1.	752	370	(yes)	no	382
2.	343	162	yes	no	
3.	476	254	yes	no	
4.	317	65	yes	no	
5.	564	283	yes	no	
6.	236	54	yes	no	
7.	643	431	yes	no	
8.	357	45	yes	no	
9.	400	251	yes	no	
10.	507	344	yes	no	

Name:

SUBTRACT 3-DIGIT NUMBERS

Subtract. Use hundreds, tens, and ones
models to help.

1.

hundreds	tens	ones
⁴	¹⁰	□
5̸	0̸	6
− 3	8	2
1	2	4

hundreds	tens	ones
□	□	□
7	3	8
− 4	5	2

2.

hundreds	tens	ones
□	□	□
3	2	9
−	7	4

hundreds	tens	ones
□	□	□
6	4	5
− 2	0	3

3.

hundreds	tens	ones
□	□	□
3	4	5
− 2	7	0

hundreds	tens	ones
□	□	
8	7	4
− 2	8	3

MORE SUBTRACTING 3-DIGIT NUMBERS

Subtract.

1.

$$\begin{array}{r} \cancel{5}\,^{5}\!\cancel{6}^{12}\,2 \\ -2\,3\,5 \\ \hline 3\,2\,7 \end{array}$$

$$\begin{array}{r} 7\,5\,3 \\ -3\,8\,1 \\ \hline \end{array}$$

$$\begin{array}{r} 3\,7\,5 \\ -1\,5\,2 \\ \hline \end{array}$$

$$\begin{array}{r} 8\,1\,6 \\ -7\,3\,5 \\ \hline \end{array}$$

$$\begin{array}{r} 4\,8\,3 \\ -2\,5\,6 \\ \hline \end{array}$$

2.

$$\begin{array}{r} 6\,2\,5 \\ -2\,5\,4 \\ \hline \end{array}$$

$$\begin{array}{r} 3\,6\,8 \\ -1\,5\,4 \\ \hline \end{array}$$

$$\begin{array}{r} 7\,8\,0 \\ -3\,5\,6 \\ \hline \end{array}$$

$$\begin{array}{r} 4\,2\,5 \\ -\quad 8 \\ \hline \end{array}$$

$$\begin{array}{r} 9\,7\,6 \\ -8\,8\,4 \\ \hline \end{array}$$

3.

$$\begin{array}{r} 8\,4\,9 \\ -5\,1\,7 \\ \hline \end{array}$$

$$\begin{array}{r} 4\,5\,0 \\ -2\,7\,0 \\ \hline \end{array}$$

$$\begin{array}{r} 6\,3\,7 \\ -3\,7\,6 \\ \hline \end{array}$$

$$\begin{array}{r} 7\,7\,7 \\ -4\,2\,4 \\ \hline \end{array}$$

$$\begin{array}{r} 9\,8\,5 \\ -6\,5\,9 \\ \hline \end{array}$$

Solve.

Workspace

4. The drama club sold 138 tickets for Monday's show. They sold 75 tickets for Tuesday's show. How many more tickets did they sell for Monday?

_____ tickets

5. Write a word problem. Use the numbers 438 and 276. Then solve the problem.

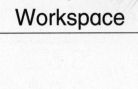
PROBLEM-SOLVING STRATEGY: SOLVE A SIMPLER PROBLEM

✔ Read
✔ Plan
✔ Solve
✔ Look Back

Solve.

Workspace

1. Amanda's music book has 332 songs. She has played all but 104 of them. How many songs has Amanda played?

_____

2. There were 92 members in the school chorus last year. There are 76 members this year. How many more members were in the chorus last year?

_____

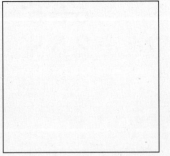

3. Dan traveled 63 miles to practice with his band. Then he traveled 63 miles back home. He did this twice in one week. How many miles did he travel?

_____

4. Two bus loads of people went to a concert. The first bus left with 93 people. The second bus left with 65 people. Then it picked up 15 more people on the way. How many people went to the concert by bus?

_____

ADD AND SUBTRACT MONEY

$3.60 $5.94 $2.18 $6.49

Solve.	Workspace
1. Tana bought a CD and a cassette tape. How much money did she spend? $8.12	$5.94 + 2.18 $8.12
2. Kevin bought a computer game. He gave the clerk $5.00. How much change did he get? _____	
3. Pat bought a video. Rita bought a CD. How much more did Pat spend than Rita? _____	
4. Paco has $7.00 to spend. He wants to buy 2 computer games. Can he afford to buy them? _____	

McGraw-Hill School Division

PROBLEM SOLVING: CHOOSE THE METHOD

✔ Read
✔ Plan
✔ Solve
✔ Look Back

Solve. Choose the best method for you.

Workspace

1. One day the orchestra traveled 327 miles. The next day it traveled 154 miles. How many miles did the orchestra travel both days?

   _____

2. It was 625 miles to the first city on the orchestra's tour. It was 433 miles to the second city. How much farther was the first city than the second city?

   _____

3. The orchestra traveled 238 miles each day for three days. How many miles did the orchestra travel in all?

   _____

4. Two cities on the orchestra's tour were 135 miles apart. The third city was 120 miles farther. How far was it to the third city?

   _____

McGraw-Hill School Division

Name: _____

MIXED REVIEW

Write how many hundreds, tens, and ones.
Write the number.

Write a 0 when there are no tens or no ones.

1.

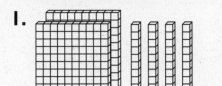

hundreds	tens	ones
2	4	1

241

2.

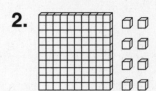

hundreds	tens	ones

_____

3.

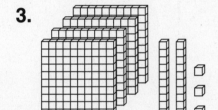

hundreds	tens	ones

_____

4.

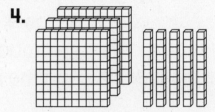

hundreds	tens	ones

_____

5.

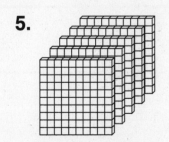

hundreds	tens	ones

_____

6.

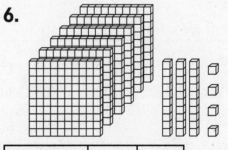

hundreds	tens	ones

_____

MULTIPLY BY 1, 2, AND 3

Use ○ and Workmat 4 if you would like.

Multiply.

1.

2 groups of __2__

2 × 2 = __4__

2.

4 groups of _____

4 × 3 = _____

3.

2 groups of _____

2 × 1 = _____

4.

5 groups of _____

5 × 3 = _____

5.

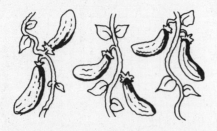

3 groups of _____

3 × 2 = _____

6.

4 groups of _____

4 × 1 = _____

MULTIPLY BY 4 AND 5

Write the multiplication sentence.
Find the product.

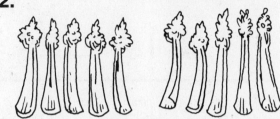
Use ⬤ and Workmat 4 if you would like.

1.

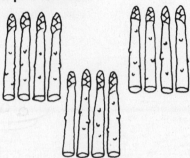

3 groups of 4

$\underline{3} \times \underline{4} = \underline{12}$

2.

2 groups of 5

____ × ____ = ____

3.

5 groups of 3

____ × ____ = ____

4.

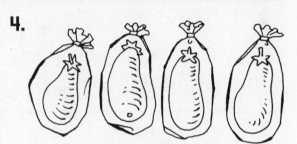

4 groups of 1

____ × ____ = ____

5.

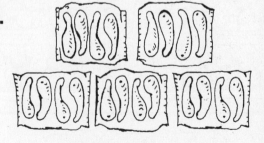

5 groups of 4

____ × ____ = ____

6.

5 groups of 5

____ × ____ = ____

MULTIPLICATION PATTERNS

Find the product.

5 x 2 = 10
factor x factor = product

1. $4 \times 1 =$ ___4___

   $1 \times 4 =$ _____

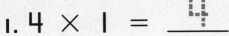

2. $3 \times 4 =$ _____

   $4 \times 3 =$ _____

3. $1 \times 2 =$ _____

   $2 \times 1 =$ _____

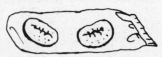

4. $5 \times 3 =$ _____

   $3 \times 5 =$ _____

5. $4 \times 5 =$ _____

   $5 \times 4 =$ _____

6. $1 \times 5 =$ _____

   $5 \times 1 =$ _____

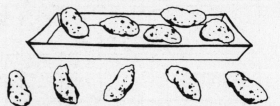

McGraw-Hill School Division

PROBLEM-SOLVING STRATEGY: MAKE A TABLE

✔ Read
✔ Plan
✔ Solve
✔ Look Back

Make a table to solve.

1. Tom makes 8 sandwiches. He puts 2 lettuce leaves on each sandwich. How many lettuce leaves does Tom need? _____ lettuce leaves

sandwiches	1	2	3							
lettuce leaves	2	4								

2. Kim makes 7 jars of carrot juice. She needs 5 carrots for each jar. How many carrots does Kim need? _____ carrots

jars of juice	1									
carrots	5	10								

3. Alec puts peanut butter on 9 celery sticks. Then he adds 4 raisins to each celery stick. How many raisins does he need? _____ raisins

celery sticks	1	2							
raisins	4								

HOW MANY GROUPS?

Use counters to make groups.
Draw dots to show the groups.
Write how many groups.

Each group must have the same number of counters.

1. Use 10 counters.
Make groups of 2.

_____ groups of 2

2. Use 8 counters.
Make groups of 4.

_____ groups of 4

3. Use 8 counters.
Make groups of 2.

_____ groups of 2

4. Use 16 counters.
Make groups of 8.

_____ groups of 8

5. Use 25 counters.
Make groups of 5.

_____ groups of 5

McGraw-Hill School Division

HOW MANY IN EACH GROUP?

Use counters to make the groups.
Draw dots to show the groups.
Write how many in each group.

Each group must have the same number of counters.

1. Use 14 counters.
   Make 2 groups.

   _____ in each group

2. Use 9 counters.
   Make 3 groups.

   _____ in each group

3. Use 18 counters.
   Make 3 groups.

   _____ in each group

4. Use 20 counters.
   Make 4 groups.

   _____ in each group

5. Use 16 counters.
   Make 4 groups.

   _____ in each group

PROBLEM SOLVING: USE MODELS

✔ Read
✔ Plan
✔ Solve
✔ Look Back

Use models to solve.

1. Karen picks 20 radishes.
She puts 4 radishes in each bunch.
How many bunches of radishes are there?

_____ bunches

2. Paul grows 6 stalks of corn.
He gets 18 ears of corn in all.
How many ears of corn are there
for each stalk?

_____ ears of corn for each stalk

3. Vicky opens 4 cans of water chestnuts.
There are 6 water chestnuts in each can.
How many water chestnuts are there
altogether?

_____ water chestnuts

4. Sam makes 4 stuffed peppers.
He puts 4 cherry tomatoes in each pepper.
How many cherry tomatoes are there in all?

_____ cherry tomatoes